COLORADO MOUNTAINS & PASSES

Short Tours in the Rockies

Sarah Wallingford MAROON BELLS

A RENAISSANCE HOUSE PUBLICATION

Silvia Pettem

2000 Printing

ISBN: 1-55838-117-1

Renaissance House Publishers
A Division of Primer Publishers
5738 North Central Avenue
Phoenix, Arizona 85012

1-800-521-9221

Cover photo of Longs Peak courtesy of Janet Robertson

10 9 8 7 6 5 4 3

Printed in Hong Kong, Published in the United States of America

Welcome

Colorado's mountains are certainly its most awesome feature. Wild, rugged, and unforgiving to the unprepared traveler, many areas of the Colorado Rockies are, nevertheless, accessible to the novice outdoorsman or the flatland motorist. This completely new and revised edition of *Colorado Mountains and Passes* offers suggestions on where to drive or hike to experience some of the finest features of the Colorado Rockies. In addition to directions and current services, there is a bit of historical background on each of the areas. In selecting mountains and passes to profile, emphasis was given to those most accessible to the average traveler.

Should you wish to know more about Colorado's spectacular mountains and passes, we suggest these fine books:

The Colorado Pass Book, by Don Koch
The Fourteeners, by Perry Eberhart and Philip Schmuck
The Great Gates, by Marshall Sprague
Jeep Trails to Colorado Ghost Towns, by Robert L. Brown
Stampede to Timberline, by Muriel Sibell Wolle
Tracking the Ghost Railroads, by Robert Ormes

Other **Renaissance Traveler** volumes of interest include:

COLORADO GEMS & MINERALS: A Guide to Native Gemstones
Day Hikes On THE COLORADO TRAIL
A Guide to Locating ROCKY MOUNTAIN WILDFLOWERS
PARKS AND MONUMENTS of New Mexico, Colorado and Utah
LOST MINES & BURIED TREASURE: A Guide to Sites & Legends of the Southwest

Silvia Pettem writes a weekly history column for the Boulder *Daily Camera* and continues to research and write on Colorado history. Her latest books are *Boulder: Evolution of a City; Inn and Around Nederland: Accommodating the Traveler Then and Now; Excursions from Peak to Peak: Then and Now; Chautauqua Centennial: A Hundred Years of Programs; Legend of a Landmark: A History of the Hotel Boulderado;* and *Separate Lives: The Story of Mary Rippon.*

Contents

Stanley Zamonski — 60-MILLION-YEAR-OLD MOUNTAINS

Geology & Mapping

The Rocky Mountains extend from northern New Mexico into Canada, a part of the great mountain chain that, with the Andes in South America, makes up the backbone of the Western Hemisphere. Of the mountains, those in Colorado are the highest. Colorado has fifty-three mountains over 14,000 feet (the Fourteeners), and more than a thousand over 10,000 feet.

Today's Rockies were formed about 60 million years ago, and at times during the next 30 million years, there was great volcanic activity in this area. Spanish Peaks, part of the San Juans, and other areas were once active volcanoes. After this volcanic period, Colorado was uplifted to its present altitude. Some activity occurred on the eastern plains, more took place under the plateaus of the west, but most of the internal movement was concentrated in the middle of the state. The land, and the streams on it, began to rise, resulting in stream-cut canyons on a high plateau.

As snow fields accumulated on the slopes and at the heads of stream-cut valleys, the snow gradually changed to ice and formed glaciers. Colorado had thousands of individual glaciers, of which no more than fifteen remain, some of those not *true* glaciers because they do not move. When the glaciers advanced from additional accumulation of ice and snow, and then

Harvey Gardiner CARVING OF A MOUNTAIN PEAK

retreated from melting and evaporation, they created many of today's mountain lakes. Their movement also carved out great U-shaped valleys, scooped out rock and dammed valleys, and deposited irregular masses known as *moraines*. In changing the valleys from V-shapes to U-shapes, some of the mountain peaks became more pointed. *Cirques*, the large natural amphitheaters along the high peaks, are where the ancient glaciers began.

Different rock structures eroded in different ways. Many of the peaks in Southwestern Colorado's San Juans are composed of volcanic rocks carved into shapes from sharp peaks to dome-shaped summits. The jagged, sawtoothed Sangre de Cristos are made up of rock like that at Colorado Springs' Garden of the Gods. The majority of Colorado's mountains are composed of igneous rocks, formed by the cooling and hardening of molten material from the earth's interior.

With the development of more accurate measuring procedures, the stated elevations of many of the peaks have changed. Their basic mapping dates from 1873 when both the Hayden and Wheeler Surveys began their work in Colorado.

The group headed by Ferdinand V. Hayden represented the United States Geological and Geographical Survey. Hayden's rival was George M. Wheeler, hired by the U.S. Department of War to do military mapping west of the hundredth meridian. Often, each group was

University of Colorado ARAPAHO GLACIER

ignorant of the other's presence, and thus duplicated research. The two surveys were completed in 1876, but since Hayden's reports were better prepared, he became better known. With Major John W. Powell and Clarence King, Hayden formed the United States Geological Survey in 1879.

The Harvard Surveyors explored and measured the Sawatch Range. All were Harvard students led by Josiah D. Whitney, for whom California's Mount Whitney is named. In keeping with its academic interests, the group named one peak Harvard, and another Yale. Columbia and Princeton were named later, constituting the Collegiate Peaks near Buena Vista.

Barriers though they were, some parts of the Colorado Rockies were easier to traverse than others. Animals took the paths of least resistance and the Indians followed them. Their dogs and horses, pulling *travois* laden with their belongings, wore the trails into more defined pathways. The mountain men followed these same routes. The peaks served as geographic reference points for explorers and surveyors, but the saddle or low point was the easiest route between them. After crossing the Continental Divide near Estes Park in the winter of 1826-27, one trapper wrote:

"The passage occurred six days, during which we had to pass along compact drifts of snow higher than a man on horseback. The narrow path through these drifts is made by the frequent passing of the buffaloes, of which we found many dead bodies in the way."

Silvia Pettem LEBANON MINE BETWEEN GEORGETOWN & SILVER PLUME

TRAVERSING THE MOUNTAINS

To weary western travelers in the mid-19th century, the Colorado Rockies were to be avoided at all costs. Those *en route* to Oregon or to the gold fields of California detoured north over Wyoming's spacious South Pass. To others, the mountains were a magnet.

The Ute Indians occupied most of Colorado's mountain region from the 16th century to the mid-19th century. Eastern trappers scrambled all over the Rockies in the 1820s and 1830s when beaver pelts were fashionable for top hats. But the first white men to see Colorado's mountains were the Spanish explorers from Santa Fe on their occasional expeditions north. After the Louisiana Purchase in 1803, when Meriwether Lewis and William Clark set out on the first official western expedition, the Rockies were on the map.

The second expedition was headed by Lieutenant Zebulon M. Pike. His mission was to follow the Arkansas River and explore the southern part of the Louisiana Purchase. Late in 1806, he discovered but did not ascend the peak that bears his name.

Major Stephen H. Long discovered the peak named for him in 1820, then headed south. Three of his men reached the summit of Pikes Peak, where botanist and physician Dr. Edwin James made the first recorded observations from the summit of a fourteener on this continent. When fashion changed the demand from beaver to silk, many trappers became guides for

Denver Public Library OPENING OF MOFFAT TUNNEL

mountain expeditions, such as those of John C. Fremont and John W. Gunnison, searching for railroad routes through the Rockies.

Until the miners arrived, most travel over the passes was on foot or horseback. After gold was discovered in Colorado in 1858, hoards of prospectors built roads over the great ranges to reach this mining wealth. Major gold discoveries were made early in 1859 in Idaho Springs, Central City and Gold Hill, all on the east side of the Front Range. Although the terrain was rough and the mountains steep, miners built crude wagon roads to bring in supplies.

Railroads next began chugging through canyons and over the Continental Divide. But Colorado's impenetrable mountains forced the Transcontinental Railroad to build through Wyoming.

The next push to make the high mountain passes fit for wagons and trains came with the discovery of rich lead and silver ore in Leadville, elevation 10,200 feet. Profit became a motive for improved toll roads.

Another major mountain barrier was eliminated in 1927 with the opening of the Moffat Tunnel, which routed trains under the Continental Divide rather than over arduous Rollins Pass. In 1973, the Eisenhower Tunnel under the Continental Divide on I-70 eliminated the need for motorists to traverse Loveland Pass.

Harvey Gardiner DIVIDE FROM JAMES PEAK

The Continental Divide

The Continental Divide is the continuous crest along the tops of the mountains that separates the water drainages of the country. But don't be fooled -- the Continental Divide is not always at the highest point in an area. Driving west over Trail Ridge Road, for example, you reach the summit at 12,183 feet, but you cross the Divide in your descent down the western side a bit further and several hundred feet lower. Travelers can "stand" upon the Continental Divide at a turnout on Trail Ridge Road in Rocky Mountain National Park or any number of well-marked sites on Colorado's mountain highways.

Rivers rising on the eastern side of the Continental Divide flow into the Gulf of Mexico. Colorado's major eastern rivers are the North and South Platte, which join as the Platte River in Nebraska, the Arkansas, and the Rio Grande. The major western slope river, the Colorado, cuts through the Arizona Grand Canyon on its way to the Pacific. Other western slope rivers include the Yampa, Dolores, and the Gunnison. Some western slope water is, however, diverted east. The Colorado Big Thompson Project, completed in 1953, annually delivers 310,000 acre-feet of Colorado River water in a 13-mile long tunnel under the Continental Divide between Grand Lake and Estes Park. Denver draws a portion of its water from Dillon Reservoir, with water from the Blue River, through a tunnel 23.3 miles long.

Stanley Zamonski

TIMBERLINE ON TRAIL RIDGE ROAD

Timberline Country

With regard to plant and animal life, every thousand feet one ascends is like going north 350 miles. In Colorado, the alpine tundra region begins at approximately 11,300 feet. This treeline becomes lower as latitude increases. From the Russian word for "land of no trees," the tundra's cold temperatures and high winds prohibit the growth of any but delicate ground-hugging plants. The growing season is limited to twelve weeks. At the lower edge of this life zone, the pines are dwarfed and deformed like crafted bonsai trees. Only a few animals make this region their home. Mountain goats, bighorn sheep, pikas and hoary marmots are among the alpine dwellers.

Weather conditions are unpredictable in the high country. Although temperatures can reach 80° F. in July, sudden thunderstorms can drop the temperature 50 degrees or more in the mountains, and bring severe lightning. Such afternoon storms are short, but frequent. By the end of August, when the first frosts occur, most of the snow from the previous winter has melted. In all seasons, travelers should guard against the intensity of the high altitude sun.

High altitude air contains less oxygen than at lower elevations. Until the body can build up more oxygen-carrying red blood cells, travelers tire easily, feel light-headed, and may have nosebleeds at high altitudes.

Harvey Gardiner LONGS PEAK (Front Range)

The Mountain Ranges

Although the Colorado Rockies rise abruptly along an approximate 105° longitude, they are not a solid mass of mountains. Generally separated into sixteen distinct ranges, each has a general unity of form, structure, and geologic age. The ranges cover an area the length of the state in a strip about one hundred miles from east to west. Each range includes its own peaks, ridges and valleys. Major ranges are the Front, Ten Mile, Mosquito, Sawatch, Elk Mountains, Sangre de Cristo, and the San Juans.

First discovered and explored was the Front Range, immediately west of Colorado's population centers. The almost flat, eroded tops of Longs Peak, Pikes Peak, and Mount Evans are thought to be the uplifted part of the same rock structure buried under the sediments on the plains. The northern end of the Front Range splits into two ridges, the Medicine Bow Mountains and the Laramie Range. At the southern end, a southwestern ridge connects the Front Range to the Wet Mountains.

Between South Park and Leadville lie the Ten Mile and Mosquito Ranges. These mountains are highly mineralized and have been extensively mined. West of Breckenridge, in the Ten Mile Range, is Quandary Peak, so named because the miners there couldn't

Harvey Gardiner MOUNT MASSIVE

determine the character of their ore. The name of Mosquito Range evolved from a mining company. As the story goes, when the owners met to sign the incorporation papers, a mosquito landed on the line left blank for the company name, so they wrote in Mosquito Mining Company. Major peaks in the area are Mounts Lincoln, Democrat, Sherman, and Bross. North of the Ten Mile are the Gore and Park ranges, Gore named in memory of Sir George Gore, the wealthy, decadent Irish hunter who roamed Colorado with Jim Bridger as his guide.

Running north and south for one hundred miles through the center of the state is the Sawatch Range, containing Colorado's four highest mountains and 15 of the 53 Fourteeners. Regarded as the watershed of the continent, Sawatch is a form of the Indian word *Saguache*, meaning "water of the blue earth." The peaks of the Sawatch are divided into three groups. Those near Leadville were named by miners, and include Massive, Elbert, La Plata, and Grizzly. Northernmost in the range is Mount of the Holy Cross, so named because snow-filled ravines on its face form a large, perfect, white cross. The collegiate group--Harvard, Columbia, Yale, and Princeton-- cluster around Buena Vista. At the southern end are Antero and Shavano, both named for Ute Indians. Aquamarines* (the state gem) are found near 14,000 feet on Mount Antero,

* See **Colorado Traveler**, *Gems & Minerals*

Stanley Zamonski MT. WILSON & WILSON'S PEAK (San Miguel Range)

making the peak a strenuous destination for gem collectors.

Hayden wrote in 1874, that the Elk Mountains (west of the Sawatch between Aspen and Crested Butte) "are probably without a parallel for ruggedness, depth, and picturesque beauty in any portion of the West." In this group are Pyramid, Capitol, Snowmass, Castle Peak, and North and South Maroon Peaks known as the Maroon Bells. The West Elk Mountains, northeast of Montrose, are a circular group of isolated peaks, most of them formed when molten rock arched into domes.

The early Spanish explorers spoke of a red hue to the mountains. As early as 1811, Spanish maps were marked "Sierra Amalgre," or Red Range, for the eastern border of the San Luis Valley. The range, known today as the Sangre de Cristo, or Blood of Christ, swings to the east at La Veta Pass west of Walsenburg, then continues as the Culebra Range straight south into New Mexico. There it suddenly ends, marking the southern limit of the Rocky Mountains. A row of sky-piercing peaks succeed one another down the entire range, culminating in Sierra Blanca, one of the most spectacular masses in the state. Other peaks include Crestone, Crestone Needle, Culebra, Old Baldy, Humboldt, and Kit Carson.

Covering most of southwestern Colorado are the San Juan Mountains. Fremont called them "the most

Harvey Gardiner — MT. PRINCETON (Sawatch Range)

impracticable of all the Rocky Mountain ranges, inaccessible to the trappers and hunters, even in summertime." He lost 11 men there in his 1848-49 expedition. Most major peaks were given different names by the Hayden and Wheeler Surveys, the U.S.G.S. ultimately selecting Hayden's. Among the highest are San Luis, Handies, Stewart, Wetterhorn, Redcloud, Mount Sneffels, Sunshine, Eolus, Sunlight, Windom, and Uncompahgre--"hot water spring" in Ute. The remaining Colorado ranges include the San Miguel, west of the San Juans, the Elkhead Range, in the north central part of the state, and Rabbit Ears Range, which divides North Park from Middle Park.

COLORADO'S MAJOR MOUNTAIN RANGES

Harvey Gardiner LONGS PEAK

Peak to Peak Highway

The Peak to Peak route along U.S. 36 recently was designated a Colorado "scenic highway." This section between Black Hawk and Ward was built in the early 1860s as a supply road between these two gold mining towns. Nederland became a freighting center after the discovery of silver in Caribou hastened the building of the Boulder Canyon road.

The road between Ward and Estes Park became widely used after the narrow gauge railroad reached Ward. Tourists piled into stagecoaches to go fishing and sightseeing. Just north of Ward is the turn-off to Red Rock and Brainard Lakes, where mountains in the Indian Peaks Wilderness Area, including Kiowa, Navajo, Pawnee, Paiute, and Mount Audubon, come into view. Other roads along the way lead to historic mining communities, from touristy Central City to the nearly deserted site of Caribou. Also in the area is Gold Hill, Colorado's first mining district, which still has a feel of the "old days."

To travel the Peak to Peak Highway from Denver, take U.S. 36 north through Boulder and Lyons to Estes Park. Go south on Colorado 7, past Mount Meeker on the right. After Allenspark there is a turn-out with a good view back to Mount Meeker and Longs Peak. At the intersection with Colorado 72 turn right. Nine miles later is the right turn to Brainard Lake. Colorado 72 continues on to Nederland. Turn right onto Colorado 119 through Black Hawk (one mile from Central City), to its end. To return to Denver, turn left on U.S. 6.

Stanley Zamonski TRAIL RIDGE ROAD

TRAIL RIDGE ROAD
(MILNER PASS)

Estes Park, eastern gateway to Rocky Mountain National Park, is connected to the west entrance at Grand Lake by Trail Ridge Road (U.S. 34). The route follows three miles along the crest of the Front Range, making it the highest continuous automobile road in America.

Trail Ridge Road is an excellent place to observe the results of glacial activity. Travelers can view valleys, canyons, meadows, glacial lakes, and the park's 76 peaks over 12,000 feet.

Most impressive is Longs Peak, the northern-most of Colorado's 14,000-foot peaks. More than 20 climbing routes, some extremely difficult, reach the 14,256-foot summit. The Longs Peak trailhead and campground is just off Colorado 7, south of Estes Park.

Conquering Longs Peak had been put into the minds of adventurers by science fiction writer Jules Verne. In his 1886 story, *From Earth to Moon*, Verne envisioned a 280-foot telescope with a 16-foot reflector on the summit of Longs Peak to track an imagined moon shot from Florida. Englishwoman Isabella Bird, who climbed the mountain in bloomers, popularized it further in *A Lady's Life in the Rocky Mountains*.

Naturalist Enos Mills, responsible for the creation of Rocky Mountain National Park, made 297 ascents of the peak, 32 in one month and six of those at night. In 1960, Dave Rearick and Bob Kamps became the first to

Stanley Zamonski ALBERTA FALLS, ROCKY MT. N.P.

climb the treacherous Diamond, the 1,000 vertical feet of granite on the east side of the peak.

Along Trail Ridge Road, life zones change from the heavy growths of fir, spruce, pine, and aspen at lower elevations, to tundra vegetation at the top. At approximately 11,000 feet, a few straggling trees mark the upper limit of the forest. Although the high point on the road is 12,183 feet, the Continental Divide is farther west at 10,759-foot Milner Pass. Nearby is a visitors' center with exhibits, films, and literature on the alpine region.

The route over Milner Pass is open only in the summer, but lower portions of the park never close. Big Elk Meadows near the north entrance is a sanctuary for elk, deer, and big horn sheep. Short trails around Bear Lake offer pleasant hikes year-round.

The town of Estes Park is accessible from Denver, Boulder, and Lyons by U.S. 36. From Greeley or Loveland, travel through the Big Thompson Canyon on U.S. 34. There are entrances to Rocky Mountain National Park via either of these routes. Gate admission includes an excellent map.

Head west on Trail Ridge Road over Milner Pass to Grand Lake, crossing the Continental Divide. For an all-day scenic loop, follow U.S. 34 to Granby. Turn left on U.S. 40, crossing the Continental Divide again at 11,313-foot Berthoud Pass. At Empire, return to Denver on eastbound I-70.

Carnegie Library EARLY HIKERS

ARAPAHO PASS

(See map #2 p. 25)

Arapaho Pass, a former Indian trail, connects the plains with Middle Park. Conceived as a possible military route, by 1900 it was still a minor wagon road, never commercially developed. Until it became popular with hikers, the only activity in the area was the Fourth of July Mine below Arapaho Peak at 11,252 feet, where silver was mined for 25 years. In Boulder, 28 miles away, no one seemed aware that the perpetual ice and snow atop Arapaho Peak was a glacier. Around the turn of the century, the city purchased the glacier and its watershed of lakes, and piped the "99.966 percent pure" water to reservoirs for its municipal supply. Today, only 10 percent of Boulder's water comes from the glacier. At one time, the Boulder Chamber of Commerce organized glacier hikes for large groups, climbs up Arapaho Peak, and climbs over Arapaho Pass.

Arapaho Pass, at 11,905 feet, can be crossed on foot. Take Colorado 119 west from Boulder to Nederland. Continue left on 119 thru town, then right on County Road 130 through Eldora--(the town, not the ski area). Go 10 miles to the end of the road at Fourth of July Campground. The trail emerges 3-1/2 miles north of Frazer on U.S. 40.

Harvey Gardiner JAMES PEAK FROM NEEDLE'S EYE TUNNEL

Rollins Pass

(See map #2 p. 25)

John Quincy Adams Rollins was the first to run a road over the Continental Divide west of Denver. An adventurous businessman and billiards player, Rollins quitely bought up hundreds of acres between Nederland and Black Hawk, and called the area Rollinsville. If he built a road from Rollinsville to Middle Park, he reasoned, his town would become a thriving tourist depot and supply center.

Rollins' toll road opened in 1873, but by then, Georgetown merchants realized that they were being by-passed and worked to open Berthoud Pass, which eventually became the major route. Rollins Pass *was* used intermittently, and in 1904, Denver financier David Moffat chose the route for the highest railroad in the country. The arduous pass route was eliminated in 1927 when the Moffat tunnel under the Continental Divide became a reality.

Near the summit of Rollins Pass are some substantial remnants of the Moffat Road, including trestles and the Needle's Eye Tunnel. Four-wheel drive vehicles can reach this tunnel from either side. But in recent years a rock slide in the tunnel has prevented a through crossing.

To reach Rollins Pass, take Colorado 119 west from Boulder to Nederland. Continue left on 119 to Rollinsville, then right at a marked dirt road to Rollins Pass.

Ed Raines RABBIT EARS RANGE FROM WEST OF CAMERON PASS

Cameron Pass

(See map #1 p. 47)

Cameron Pass crosses the Continental Divide just north of Milner Pass. But the mountains here are lower and the old toll-road-turned highway is an easy drive. The beginning of the route follows the Cache la Poudre River, where French fur trappers once stashed their powder kegs to lighten their loads.

About half way up, the river canyon turns to a glacier valley. A wagon road to the left near the top once took stage coaches from Fort Collins to the short-lived mining town of Lulu City. Mount Richthofen, at 12,940 feet, the high point of the Never Summer Range, is the most prominent peak at the top of this 10,285-foot pass.

The route descends into the old Indian hunting grounds of North Park. Nearby Walden has supplied the White House with its Christmas tree.

To travel Cameron Pass from Fort Collins, take U.S. 287 north to Teds Place where Colorado 14 heads west. Follow this route up Poudre Canyon, over Cameron Pass to Walden. For a circle trip continue north on Colorado 125, turning right onto Colorado 127. This road heads into the Medicine Bow Mountains and becomes Wyoming 230 to Laramie. U.S 287 is a downhill drive to Fort Collins.

University of Colorado RABBIT EARS PASS

RABBIT EARS AND GORE PASSES

Early settlers, attracted to the rhythmic chugging of mineral hot springs, named their town Steamboat Springs. Now known for its skiing, Steamboat Springs is reached by crossing the Continental Divide at 9,680 feet over Rabbit Ears Pass, named for the hundred-foot high twin pinnacles on Rabbit Ears Peak. They can be seen on the east side from Walden to Kremmling.

Southeast of Rabbit Ears Pass is 9,527-foot Gore Pass, the original route between Middle Park and the Yampa River valley. It was named for English sportsman, Sir George Gore, the legendary hunter who roamed the area in the 1850s. He is said to have slaughtered 3,000 bison, 40 grizzly bears, and unknown numbers of elk and deer. Gore supposedly discovered gold in the area, too, but kept his findings secret because he feared that his men would desert the hunting expedition for the lure of gold.

From Empire on I-70, take U.S. 40 over Berthoud Pass to Granby. This pass was constructed as a trade route into Middle Park. Cold winter air settles into Fraser on the northern side, giving it the dubious nickname "icebox of the nation." Continue on U.S. 40 through Kremmling, over Muddy and Rabbit Ears Passes into Steamboat Springs.

To return, go south on Colorado 131 through the Yampa River valley to Tonopas. Turn left on Colorado 134, over Gore Pass to Kremmling, and south on Colorado 9 past Green Mountain Reservoir to I-70 at Dillon.

Stanley Zamonski MONARCH PASS

MARSHALL PASS

(See map #4 p. 25)

This gentle 10,846-foot route over the Continental Divide follows the railroad grade of the narrow-gauge Denver & Rio Grande. It was discovered by Lt. William L. Marshall of the army's Wheeler Survey in 1873. While in the San Juans, Marshall developed a severe toothache and decided to find the most direct way back to Denver--and a dentist.

The route soon became a toll road. In 1881 it brought the first railroad into Gunnison and to western slope mines. Near the summit are some dilapidated snowsheds and building foundations from the railroad which was abandoned in 1955.

Dominating the view to the northeast is 13,971-foot Mount Ouray, the southern point of the Sawatch Range. The glacier-carved cirque on the east face resembles a huge chair. Legend claims that the spirit of its namesake, Ute Indian Chief Ouray, sits and watches everything below.

To reach the pass, go west on U.S. 50 from Salida to Poncha Springs and turn left onto U.S. 285. Before the summit of Poncha Pass, turn right onto the Marshall Pass Road. The road ends at Sargents, an old stage stop and railroad depot. Turn right onto U.S. 50, and return over Monarch Pass.

James C. Ratte WHEELER GEOLOGIC AREA

Creede/Cochetopa Pass

(See map #5 p. 48)

The silver mining town of Creede in 1892 was immortalized by Cy Warman's poem, "It's Day all Day in the Daytime, and There is No Night in Creede." Bat Masterson, Bob Ford, and Soapy Smith were some of its colorful characters. Impressive mining buildings perched on steep canyon walls demand a short detour up West Willow Creek behind the town. To get there from Salida, take U.S. 285 south through Saguache. Turn right on Colorado 112. At South Fork, go right on Colorado 149 to Creede and the mining district.

Northeast of Creede in the La Garita Wilderness is the Wheeler Geologic area. Its unusual rock formations include spires, domes, pinnacles, caves, cliffs, and canyons. From Creede, continue on Colorado 149 to Slumgullion Pass. Just after the summit turn right for Los Pinos and Cochetopa Passes.

Although the Los Pinos Pass area lacks the grandeur of the San Juan crossings, the route is scenic and pleasant. Along the way is the old Los Pinos Indian Agency, now used by the Forest Service. The agency was established in 1869 when certain Utes were relocated from the San Luis Valley.

Cochetopa means "pass of the buffalo" in Ute. A low 10,030 feet over the Continental Divide, Cochetopa Pass was the natural crossing for animals and early residents. Lt. John Fremont scouted here for a railroad route but was turned back by heavy snows. The pass is a gentle climb with a good view back to the west of the San Juans rising above Lake City. To return to Salida continue on this road to Colorado 114. Turn right toward Saguache where you pick up U.S. 285.

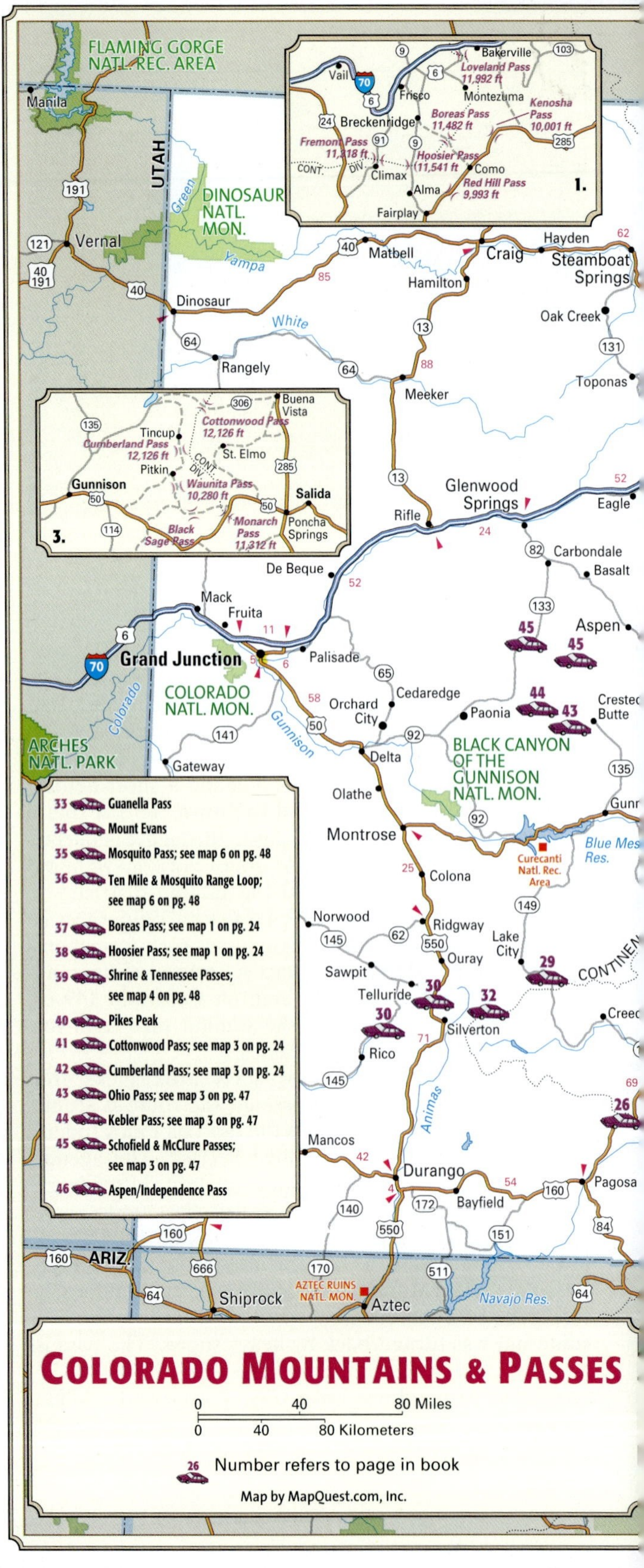

COLORADO MOUNTAINS & PASSES

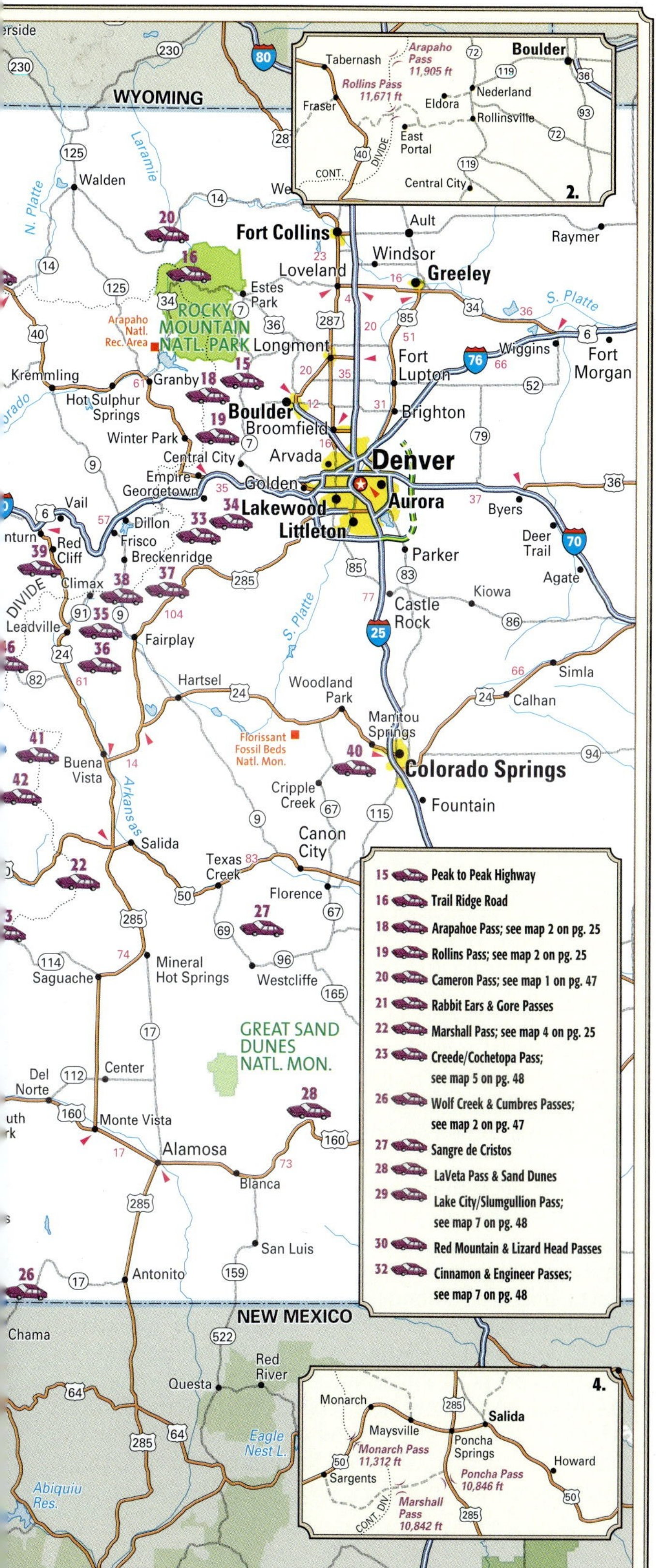
WYOMING
NEW MEXICO
Fort Collins
Loveland
Windsor
Greeley
Ault
Raymer
Estes Park
ROCKY MOUNTAIN NATL. PARK
Arapaho Natl. Rec. Area
Longmont
Fort Lupton
Wiggins
Fort Morgan
Kremmling
Granby
Hot Sulphur Springs
Boulder
Broomfield
Brighton
Winter Park
Central City
Arvada
Denver
Empire
Georgetown
Golden
Lakewood
Aurora
Littleton
Byers
Vail
Dillon
Frisco
Red Cliff
Breckenridge
Climax
Leadville
Fairplay
Parker
Deer Trail
Agate
Kiowa
Castle Rock
Simla
Calhan
Hartsel
Woodland Park
Manitou Springs
Colorado Springs
Florissant Fossil Beds Natl. Mon.
Buena Vista
Cripple Creek
Fountain
Salida
Canon City
Texas Creek
Florence
Mineral Hot Springs
Westcliffe
Saguache
GREAT SAND DUNES NATL. MON.
Del Norte
Center
Monte Vista
Alamosa
Blanca
San Luis
Antonito
Chama
Questa
Red River
Eagle Nest L.
Abiquiu Res.
Walden
Laramie
N. Platte
S. Platte
Arkansas
DIVIDE
2.
Tabernash
Arapaho Pass 11,905 ft
Boulder
Rollins Pass 11,671 ft
Fraser
Eldora
Nederland
Rollinsville
East Portal
Central City
CONT. DIVIDE
4.
Monarch
Maysville
Salida
Monarch Pass 11,312 ft
Poncha Springs
Sargents
Poncha Pass 10,846 ft
Howard
Marshall Pass 10,842 ft
CONT. DIV.
15 Peak to Peak Highway
16 Trail Ridge Road
18 Arapahoe Pass; see map 2 on pg. 25
19 Rollins Pass; see map 2 on pg. 25
20 Cameron Pass; see map 1 on pg. 47
21 Rabbit Ears & Gore Passes
22 Marshall Pass; see map 4 on pg. 25
23 Creede/Cochetopa Pass; see map 5 on pg. 48
26 Wolf Creek & Cumbres Passes; see map 2 on pg. 47
27 Sangre de Cristos
28 LaVeta Pass & Sand Dunes
29 Lake City/Slumgullion Pass; see map 7 on pg. 48
30 Red Mountain & Lizard Head Passes
32 Cinnamon & Engineer Passes; see map 7 on pg. 48

Stanley Zamonski FROM WOLF CREEK PASS

Wolf Creek and Cumbres Passes

(See map #2 p. 47)

Although Wolf Creek Pass is in southern Colorado and only 10,850 feet, this Continental Divide crossing receives an average of 600 inches of snow per year. To the west are views of the San Juans. Just south of the pass is Treasure Mountain, named for the millions of dollars in gold bullion supposedly buried there in 1790 by French explorers. The pass was recently immortalized in a country tune by C.W. McCall. To reach Wolf Creek via a scenic route from Alamosa, take U.S. 160 west. Just before Pagosa Springs, go south on U.S. 84 to Chama, New Mexico.

Recently the Cumbres & Toltec Scenic Railroad resumed operation between Chama and Antonito on a section of the historic Denver & Rio Grande narrow gauge route that reached Durango in 1881. The 64 miles of track curl above and below the road several times north of Chama. At the summit of 10,022-foot Cumbres Pass they converge with an old toll road.

Colorado 17 north traverses Cumbres and La Manga Passes to Antonito. U.S. 285 north returns to Alamosa. An alternative route heads left after La Manga Pass on a gravel road over Stunner Pass to the mining towns of Platoro and Summitville, past Conejos Peak. This road joins U.S. 160 just west of Del Norte.

Stanley Zamonski ROYAL GORGE

Sangre de Cristos

Wet Mountains and Royal Gorge

Crestone Needle and Kit Carson, Humboldt, and Creston Peaks, all Fourteeners, form a dramatic backdrop for Silver Cliff and Westcliffe in the Wet Mountain Valley. These and other mountains of the Sangre de Cristo range come into view at Hardscrabble Pass, a 9,000-foot point between Wetmore and Westcliffe. The adventurous can see them close-up from Hermit Pass, a four-wheel-drive road from Westcliffe to the San Luis Valley.

The discovery of silver had made Silver Cliff Colorado's third largest city by 1880. The next year the Denver & Rio Grande carved through the Royal Gorge to Westcliffe (where "Cat Ballou" was filmed). The world's highest suspension bridge now spans the Royal Gorge, 1,055 feet above the Arkansas River. This deep canyon also can be traversed in an aerial tramway, or seen at water level via an incline railway.

This tour follows Colorado 115 from Colorado Springs or U.S. 50 from Pueblo to Florence. Go south on Colorado 67 which becomes Colorado 96 to Westcliffe. Turn north on Colorado 69 to U.S. 50 east. At Parkdale take the side road to Royal Gorge then return to U.S. 50.

Stanley Zamonski — SAND DUNES

La Veta Pass

Great Sand Dunes Natl Monument

La Veta Pass, at 9,383-feet, followed the roadbed of the Denver & Rio Grande Railroad until a new section of highway bypassed part of this historic route. Veta is Spanish for "vein," in reference to coal in the area. The twin Spanish Peaks are to the south. To reach the pass turn west from Walsenburg on U.S. 160.

Seemingly out of place in Colorado are the Great Sand Dunes. To visit them continue on 160 through Fort Garland to Colorado 150 north. Over the course of 15,000 years, winds blowing toward the northeast across the San Luis Valley deposited sand at the foot of the Sangre de Cristo Mountains. The sand--actually eroded bits and pieces of the San Juan Mountains and glacial debris-- was carried downstream by the Rio Grande River. When the river changed its course, the sand was picked up and carried by the wind. The dunes cover 55 square miles. Rising nearly 700 feet, they are the tallest in North America.

Great Sand Dunes National Monument has a visitors' center and campground. Towering overhead are three Fourteeners--Mount Lindsey, Little Bear Peak, and Blanca Peak. Ridges run from the summit of Blanca Peak in six directions. Its north face cradles the southernmost glacier in North America. Snow habitually covers the top; hence "Blanca," Spanish for "white."

For a different return trip, go west on U.S. 160 to Alamosa, then north on Colorado 17 which joins U.S. 285 to Poncha Springs. Here U.S. 50 heads west to Pueblo.

Ed Raines LAKE SAN CRISTOBAL FROM SLUMGULLION PASS

LAKE CITY/SLUMGULLION PASS

(See map #7 p. 48)

Lake City, the only town in Hinsdale County, is a summer resort known for its fishing. In the early days it was a mining town and important junction for transportation companies serving the many San Juan mines. Susan B. Anthony lectured here promoting women's rights. In the 1870's, big Concord coaches rumbled down Slumgullion Pass on their 31-hour supply routes from La Veta near Walsenburg. At the foot of the pass is the grave where accused cannibal Alferd Packer's victims were buried.

The view from Windy Point, near the top of the 11,361-foot pass, includes Redcloud, Sunshine, Uncompahgre, and Wetterhorn Peaks, all Fourteeners in the vicinity of Cinnamon and Engineer Passes. At 14,309 feet, Uncompahgre is the highest mountain in the San Juan Range. Far below is Lake San Cristobal. The lake was formed about 800 years ago when a four-mile-long mud flow dammed the Lake Fork River. Also from Windy Point is a good view of the head wall where the slide originated.

To reach the pass, go west from Gunnison on U.S. 50, then south on Colorado 149 to Lake City. Continue on Colorado 149 past Windy Point.

To return to Gunnison, take the road which turns off to the left just below the summit. In approximately 15 miles, turn left to the town of Powderhorn and Colorado 149.

Univ. of Colorado RED MOUNTAIN PASS

Red Mountain and Lizard Head Passes

This loop takes in the heart of the San Juans, with its rugged mountains and historic mining towns. Durango began as a railroad supply point for the surrounding mines. Silverton ("silver by the ton") was united with the outside world in 1882 when the Durango & Rio Grande narrow gauge railroad reached the isolated mining town. Today the steam-powered tourist railroad still runs between the two towns.

Residents of Ouray decided that if their town was to grow, they needed a road to Silverton. Otto Mears, the short, dapper, and indomitable Russian who, five years earlier had built Marshall Pass and other toll roads, started on the 23-mile route of Red Mountain Pass. Workmen were lowered down the canyon's walls to 600 feet above the floor. There they blasted dynamite with extra-long fuses so they could be hoisted up before each explosion. The road's construction costs ran $10,000 per mile, suggesting the name Million Dollar Highway. Some say that it was named for its cost; others because it was made of gold-bearing gravel.

Red Mountain Pass crosses the Continental Divide on U.S. 550 between Silverton and Ouray. At 12,200 feet, it has more than 20 major avalanche paths. One slide path, the Riverside, has claimed six lives since

Harvey Gardiner MT. SNEFFELS

1906. Snow is a problem, even in summer. On July 6, 1888, an avalanche blocked the road at 11,008 feet, requiring a tunnel to be constructed for wagon traffic. Before coming into Ouray, this scenic highway crosses a bridge over Bear Creek Falls, 227 feet below.

At Ridgway, turn south and west onto Colorado 62. En route to Placerville is Dallas Divide, offering a breathtaking view of 14,150-foot Mount Sneffels. At Placerville, take Colorado 145 toward Telluride. This mining town turned ski town is located in a narrow valley blocked on the east by Ingram Peak and a massive ridge of mountains. Four-wheel drives can reach the town via Ophir Pass from Silverton, Black Bear Pass (from near the top of Red Mountain Pass), or Imogene Pass (from Ouray). The alternative is the following tour, which follows a longer route on main roads.

Between Telluride and Rico, a 350-foot volcanic outcrop said to resemble a lizard, looms up at Lizard Head Pass. The road roughly parallels the grade of the old Rio Grande Southern railroad. From 1931 to 1951, gasoline-powered vehicles called Galloping Geese were fitted to ride the narrow gauge rails with mail and passengers. Beyond Rico lies Dolores, home of the Anasazi Heritage Center. To complete the circuit, return to Durango on U.S. 160 east.

Ed Raines UP S. HENSON CREEK TOWARD ENGINEER PASS

Cinnamon and Engineer Passes

(Four Wheel Drive)

(See map #7 p. 48)

Cinnamon and Engineer Passes were principal routes over the San Juans for the prospectors, miners, and suppliers of such mining towns as Animas Forks, Whitecross, Mineral Point, and Capitol City of the 1870s and 1880s.

From Silverton follow the Animas River on Colorado 110 to Animas Forks. Turn right. About two miles below the 12,600-foot summit of Cinnamon Pass on the east is a turn-off south to American Basin with a close-up look at 14,048-foot Handies Peak. Further down at the site of Whitecross are excellent views of Redcloud and Sunshine Peaks, also Fourteeners.

Lake San Cristobal will be on the right shortly before reaching the well-preserved mining town and National Historic District of Lake City, where it's time to head uphill again. Go due west along Henson Creek to Capitol City and the historic stage station called Rose's Cabin. Head north and west toward 12,800-foot Engineer Pass. From the top is a view of many of the giants of the San Juans, including Wetterhorn, Engineer, Redcloud, Coxcomb and Uncompahgre Peaks. Follow the road down Mineral Creek to U.S. 550 south of Ouray. Turn left for Red Mountain Pass to go back to Silverton.

Ed Raines SAWTOOTH AND MT BIERSTADT FROM GUANELLA PASS

GUANELLA PASS

A drive over Guanella Pass can be done easily in an afternoon from the Denver area. Stop first in the old mining town of Georgetown which dates from the 1864 silver discoveries. Unlike many early towns, Georgetown escaped a major fire. Over 200 original buildings, fine examples of Victorian architecture, still stand. A steam-powered train takes visitors over the reconstructed Georgetown Loop to nearby Silver Plume. An impressive arrangement of loops and trestles makes the 700-foot climb between the two towns.

Guanella Pass is named for road builder, Byron Guanella descendent of an early Georgetown family. As the road begins to climb there is a good view of the town. Three miles up is the turn-off for Argentine Pass and the site of the silver mining camp of Waldorf. The turn-off joins the grade of the Argentine Central, the railroad which took tourists and supplies up McClellan Mountain in the mining days.

At the 11,500-foot summit of Guanella Pass are the trailheads to Sawtooth Mountain and Mount Bierstadt which stand impressively to the east. Mount Evans is just behind them, but out of view.

From Denver take 1-70 to Georgetown. Go west through the main part of town where a sign marks the route. After the summit, descend to Grant on U.S. 285. Go east through Bailey and Conifer to Denver.

Stanley Zamonski — THE ROAD UP MOUNT EVANS

Mount Evans

For spectacular scenery a short drive from Denver, nothing can beat Mount Evans. The highest paved road in North America winds its way almost to the top of this 14,264-foot peak. The view from the summit, a five-minute climb from the road, extends from Longs Peak south to Pike's Peak, with the Sangre de Cristo Range further south. Also prominent to the west are Grays and Torreys Peaks, both over 14,000 feet. The view to the east takes in Denver and the plains. Watch for shaggy, white Rocky Mountain goats who live near the top of Mount Evans and peer over the rocks like Cheshire cats. Big horn sheep are not unusual either.

The most prominent peak to the west is 14,060-foot Mount Bierstadt, named for painter Albert Bierstadt who used Mount Evans as the model for his classic painting, *Storm in the Rocky Mountains*. Bierstadt, who was the first to climb Mount Evans, originally named it Mount Rosalie for his wife. In 1870, the mountain was renamed to honor John Evans, Colorado's second territorial governor. A nearby peak to the southeast became Mount Rosalie.

To reach Mount Evans take I-70 to Idaho Springs. Exit on Colorado 103 to Echo Lake. Turn right on Colorado 5 for the 14-mile drive to the summit. Returning to Echo Lake, turn right on Colorado 103 over Squaw Pass through Bergen Park. You rejoin I-70 at the El Rancho exit.

Harvey Gardiner

MOUNT LINCOLN

Mosquito Pass

(Four Wheel Drive)

(See map #6 p. 48)

When the silver rush began in Leadville in 1878, the most direct route from South Park was over Mosquito Pass. The road established Leadville as a major mining center but was heavily used only until 1880 when the railroad pushed up the Arkansas Valley from Buena Vista. The pass was abandoned for many years. In 1949, Leadville and Fairplay residents improved the road for their first World's Championship Mosquito Pass Pack Burro Race.

At 13,188 feet, Mosquito Pass is the highest through crossing in North America. From the summit you can view the entirety of the Colorado Rockies, from Mount Sopris and Grand Mesa (west of the Elk Range), to Pikes Peak and the Great Plains on the east. Highest peak in the Mosquito Range is Mount Lincoln, north of the pass. In the same area are Mount Bross and Mount Democrat. Also at the summit is a monument to Rev. John L. "Father" Dyer who regularly traversed the pass carrying mail, gold, and the word of God.

From Frisco follow Colorado 9 through Breckenridge over Hoosier Pass to Alma. Turn west on the Mosquito Pass road. It forks left, past the ghost town of Park City to the South London mine, then goes over the pass and down to Leadville. Take Colorado 91 over Fremont Pass back to I-70.

Harvey Gardiner MT. ELBERT

Ten Mile and Mosquito Range Loop

(See map #6 p. 48)

This tour crosses the Continental Divide twice through some of the state's most heavily mineralized mountains. Gold was discovered in Breckenridge and Fairplay in 1859, in Oro City (near Leadville) in 1860, and silver brought the rush to Leadville in 1879.

Head south from I-70 at Frisco over Hoosier Pass and down U.S. 285 to Buena Vista. This ranching community boomed when the railroad came through with supplies for busy Leadville. Named "Buena Vista" for its beautiful view, it offers the dramatic backdrop of the Collegiate Range to the west.

Southwest of the town is Mount Princeton. According to local legend, Spanish conquistadores hid their treasures somewhere on the white chalk cliffs of this mountain's southern slope. To the north are Mount Yale, Mount Columbia, Mount Harvard, and Mount Oxford, named by the first mining school graduates of Harvard University.

In Buena Vista take U.S. 24 north along the Arkansas River, reaching Leadville after a climb of 2,000 feet. Dominating the western horizon from Leadville are Colorado's highest mountains: Mount Elbert at 14,433 feet and Mount Massive, 14,421 feet. Return to I-70 on Colorado 91 over Fremont Pass.

Ed Raines

QUANDARY PEAK & TEN-MILE RANGE FROM BOREAS PASS

Boreas Pass

(See map #1 p. 24)

Boreas (Greek for "rude north wind") Pass begins at Como. It is accessible from the Denver area via U.S. 285 south over Kenosha Pass. At one time this active railroad center saw 26 trains each day. The stone portion of the old roundhouse still stands. In 1882, tracks were laid for the narrow gauge Denver, South Park & Pacific over Boreas Pass to the gold-mining centers at Breckenridge and Leadville.

Tracks were abandoned in 1937. Today's road covers much of the original grade. Approaching the summit on the left is a good view of Mount Silverheels, named for a dance-hall girl who nursed smallpox victims in the mining camp of Buckskin Joe. At 11,481 feet on the Continental Divide is the old Boreas depot.

Descending on the west side is a view of 14,264-foot Quandary Peak on the left, with the high peaks of the Ten Mile Range spreading out to the north. Breckenridge Ski Area is also plainly visible. Part way down is a wooden water tank which supplied the steam engines.

The Boreas Pass Road leads into Breckenridge. A scenic return route goes past Keystone and Arapaho Basin Ski Areas and over Loveland Pass. Turn right onto Swan Mountain Road outside Breckenridge just before Dillon Reservoir. At its end, turn right onto U.S. 6. Loveland Pass is an easy-to-drive paved highway with a panorama of the central mountain area from the top. If time is crucial, get on I-70 at Frisco and take the Eisenhower Tunnel under the Continental Divide to return to Denver.

Silvia Pettem

SOUTH PARK FROM KENOSHA PASS

Hoosier Pass

(See map #1 p. 24)

When in 1844 John Charles Fremont, with Kit Carson as his guide, crossed what would later be named Hoosier Pass, it already was known to trappers and hunters in the area. After gold was discovered in Breckenridge in 1859, prospectors climbed over Georgia Pass to reach South Park. But it wasn't long before they began to use Boreas and Hoosier Passes as well.

While slightly longer (in miles only) than the Boreas Pass trip, this excursion covers similar territory, and is all on paved roads. From Denver, head south on U.S. 285. Just west of Grant is the portal of the 23-mile Harold D. Roberts Tunnel, which carries water from Dillon Reservoir to Denver. Cross over Kenosha Pass and the large expanse of South Park opens up before you. Mount Guyot is the outstanding peak to the northwest.

After Red Hill Pass, turn right on Colorado 9 at Fairplay, settled by prospectors who were tired of claim jumpers. At Fairplay is South Park City Museum, a reconstruction of an early gold mining town.

Hoosier Pass crosses the Continental Divide between Fairplay and Breckenridge on Colorado 9 at a height of 11,541 feet. To the west are Quandary Peak and Mount Lincoln. Lincoln, the highest peak in the Mosquito Range, was named for then-President Abraham Lincoln. To the east is Mount Silverheels. Continue through Breckenrigde to Frisco. Return to Denver over Loveland Pass (U.S. 6) or I-70.

Stanley Zamonski MOUNT OF THE HOLY CROSS

SHRINE AND TENNESSEE PASSES

(See map #4 p. 48)

Shrine Pass is so-named because it gives a good but distant view of 14,005-foot Mount of the Holy Cross. To view the peak close-up requires a climb up Notch Mountain southwest of Minturn. This elusive mountain received notoriety from its snow-filled crevasses which form a huge cross, although rockslides in recent years have made it less perfect. The mountain has been featured by artist Thomas Moran, poet Henry Wadsworth Longfellow, and photographer William Henry Jackson, a member of the Hayden Survey.

Mount of the Holy Cross can be seen by car 3-1/2 miles from exit 190 off I-70 on Shrine Pass Road. For many years this was the main route to Glenwood Springs and Grand Junction. High point of the drive is at 11,050 feet. The town of Redcliff is at the bottom.

From Redcliff, go south on U.S. 24. Between Redcliff and Tennessee Pass, to the east, is the site of Camp Hale. Here the army trained ski troops during World War II for its famous Tenth Mountain Division. Only the foundations of the buildings remain. At Leadville, go north on Colorado 91 over Fremont Pass to return to I-70.

Stanley Zamonski   PIKES PEAK FROM GARDEN OF THE GODS

PIKES PEAK

So inspired was Katharine Lee Bates by the view from the top of Pikes Peak in 1893, that she wrote the words for the patriotic tribute *America the Beautiful*. Zebulon Pike, for whom the mountain is named, first estimated its elevation to be 18,581 feet. Although his measurements were way off, Pikes Peak looms 14,110 feet, 1-1/2 miles above Colorado Springs, and higher from its base than any other Colorado mountain.

Edwin James, in the Long expedition of 1820, made the first recorded climb. Julia H. Holmes, immortalized in the book *A Bloomer Girl on Pikes Peak*, was the first woman to reach the top in 1858. Although the mountain prompted the slogan "Pikes Peak or Bust," little gold was found in the area until the Cripple Creek bonanza many years later.

Hiking trails were improved in the 1870s, and a meteorological observatory erected in 1876. A carriage road and cog railway were built in the late 1880s, and an automobile road in 1915.

Today, drivers race up the 18-mile road every July 4th in the Pikes Peak Hill Climb. The Cog Railway runs daily in the summer. To reach the Pikes Peak Auto Road, take U.S. 24 west from Colorado Springs up Ute Pass--one of five Ute Passes in Colorado. Turn west at Cascade for the drive to the summit.

Harvey Gardiner

COTTONWOOD PASS

Cottonwood Pass

(See map #3 p. 24)

Gunnison County mining camps sprang up quickly with an overflow of prospectors from Leadville. Cottonwood Pass over the Continental Divide soon became the major thoroughfare for bringing in supplies, even from as far as Aspen. The 14,000-foot peaks of Mount Yale to the north and Mount Princeton to the south are part of the panoramic view of the Collegiate group in the Sawatch Range.

After years of neglect, the U.S. Forest Service has reopened the 12,126-foot pass. Here is the most direct and most scenic route between Gunnison and Buena Vista. This drive takes in more passes in one day than any of the others. (See the Cumberland Tour for information on Cumberland Pass.) Waunita Pass known for its thermal springs, and Black Sage Pass are much more gentle. Monarch Pass is a U.S. highway, while Old Monarch Pass is a dirt road.

To begin the tour take Colorado 306 west from Buena Vista over Cottonwood Pass to Taylor Reservoir. Turn left and left again to Tincup. Continue south over Cumberland Pass to Pitkin. Turn left for Waunita Pass and Black Sage Pass. For Old Monarch Pass go straight, meeting U.S. 50 on the east side of Monarch Pass. A right turn brings you to U.S. 50 west of Monarch Pass. Cross the pass and turn left on U.S. 285 at Poncha Springs to return to Buena Vista.

Jeff Wingerter — SUMMIT OF CUMBERLAND PASS

Cumberland Pass

(See map #3 p. 24)

A pack trail turned wagon road was cut over Cumberland Pass in 1882 to connect the Denver, South Park & Pacific Railroad at Pitkin with the new mining camp of Tincup. Legend states that an early prospector scooped up gold, along with water, in his tin drinking cup. Although the town once supported 20 saloons, only a quiet summer community survives today.

At 12,200 feet, Cumberland Pass is one of the highest passes in Colorado suitable for passenger cars. Following the Willow Creek valley, are a series of switchbacks and a long shelf road that leads to a barren windswept summit. Several sizeable mines near the top once produced rich gold ore. Numerous 4-wheel-drive side roads lead to these mining sites, mills, and cabins on both sides of the ridge. The view to the east and north includes Mount Antero (known for its aquamarines) and other "fourteeners" in the Sawatch Range. To the northwest, beyond Taylor Park, are the Elk Mountains.

From Gunnison, take Colorado 135 north to Almont, then go right past Taylor Park Reservoir and right again to Tincup. Then go south over Cumberland Pass to Pitkin, and back through the town of Ohio to U.S. 50. Turn right to go back to Gunnison.

Stanley Zamonski CRESTED BUTTE

OHIO PASS

(GOTHIC & CRESTED BUTTE)

(See map #3 p. 47)

Crested Butte was settled when coal prospectors discovered a deposit of anthracite, much less common than the softer bituminous coal. Turn-of-the-century mining buildings have since earned the town national historic designation status. Today 12,162-foot Mount Crested Butte has made the town a prospering ski resort.

Travel north from Gunnison on Colorado 135 to the fork, turning left toward Baldwin on the Ohio Creek Road. En route to 10,000-foot Ohio Pass is an excellent view of the West Elk Mountains. From Ohio Pass, travelers can see "the Castles," unusual rock formations eroded from volcanic debris. At Lake Irwin take the right fork to Crested Butte which is in a U-shaped valley gouged by glaciers once 500 to 1,000 feet thick.

Follow Colorado 327 to Gothic, a town founded on rich wire silver. Gothic was once home to nearly 5000 people and was visited by former President Ulysses S. Grant. The Rocky Mountain Biological Laboratory, in Gothic since 1928, is used by scientists and students studying animals, birds, and flowers. Return to Crested Butte and take Colorado 135 back to Gunnison. An alternate trip for hardy 4WD'ers is the steep, rough, but very scenic Schofield Pass route (see p. 45).

National Park Service BLACK CANYON OF THE GUNNISON

Kebler Pass

(See map #3 p. 47)

The low (10,000-foot) but scenic passes in the West Elk Mountains were once part of an extensive Ute Indian trail through the Colorado Rockies into northeastern Utah. Mining led to further development. Between Ohio and Kebler Passes is a turn-off to the gold and silver mining camps of Ruby and Irwin.

As in the previous tour, take Colorado 135 north from Gunnison, then follow the Ohio Creek Road to Ohio Pass. At Lake Irwin, take the left fork to Kebler Pass. Carbon Peak, then the Anthracite Range, and West Beckwith Peak come into view from Kebler Pass. The West Elks are known for extraordinary cliffs and pinnacles. Much of the region is a wilderness area.

This tour continues through Colorado's orchards, with a side trip to the Black Canyon of the Gunnison National Monument. The gorge is about 1,300 feet wide at the rim and 2,700 feet deep, and is named for its dark rocks and deep shadows. The Utes considered it the home of evil spirits.

At Paonia Reservoir turn left on Colorado 133, then left again at Hotchkiss on Colorado 92. Go through Crawford (turn-off to the north rim of the Black Canyon of the Gunnison) to U.S. 50 which returns to Gunnison.

Denver Public Library MARBLE

SCHOFIELD & McCLURE PASSES

(Four Wheel Drive)

(See map #3 p. 47)

Schofield Pass is not a passenger car road and even requires skilled handling of a 4WD vehicle through the area known as the Devil's Punchbowl on the west side. Legend says that when the Ute Indians were driven out they placed a curse on the Crystal River Canyon which motorists would do well to respect.

Take Kebler Pass route (p. 44) from Gunnison to Paonia Reservoir. Turn right onto Colorado 133 over McClure Pass, then right again at the turn to Marble. Marble from the Yule Quarry near the town of Marble, was used in the Tomb of the Unknown Soldier in Arlington, Virginia, and in the Lincoln Memorial in Washington, D.C.

From Marble, follow the 4WD Schofield Pass Road to Gothic. A few miles up Schofield Pass after a steep, rough shelf road is Crystal, founded on silver and gold. The Lead King powerhouse (Crystal Mill) is one of the most photographed historic buildings in Colorado.

Gothic, on the eastern side of the 10,700-foot summit near Crested Butte, was an important mining camp and supply point for prospectors in the 1880s. Even then traffic over Schofield Pass was heavy, with supplies coming into the mining communities from Carbondale and Glenwood Springs. From Gothic, return to Crested Butte and to Gunnison on Colorado 135.

Stanley Zamonski MAROON BELLS

ASPEN / INDEPENDENCE PASS

The road to Independence Pass lies between Colorado's first and fifth highest mountains--Mount Elbert and La Plata Peak. At 14,433 feet, Mount Elbert is the third highest in the U.S. after Alaska's Mount McKinley and California's Mount Whitney. Travelers can reach Aspen from Glenwood Springs via Colorado 82.

At the top of Independence Pass (12,095 feet) where the road crosses the Continental Divide, Mount Elbert is visible to the east. To the left is Mount Massive. A total of 15 Fourteeners are located here in the Sawatch Range, the highest range in Colorado.

Cirques and rounded U-shaped valleys are evidence of the creeping glaciers which dramatically shaped the landscape. The Roaring Fork Braille Trail at the summit gives self-guided tours for the blind.

Aspen, now a skiing playground for the rich and famous, began as a silver mining town and quickly boomed. The largest silver nugget ever discovered in the world--2,060 pounds--came from the Smuggler mine in 1894. Today shuttle buses take visitors to Maroon Bells near Aspen. These twin peaks are the most photographed of Colorado's Fourteeners.

Colorado 82 continues east to U.S. 24. Go north here to Leadville over Tennessee Pass to I-70. For a 4WD alternative, turn left at Leadville to Hagerman Pass which goes over the tunnels of the old standard-gauge Colorado Midland Railroad. The remainder of the route follows the grade to Basalt. Turn right here to return to Glenwood on Colorado 82.

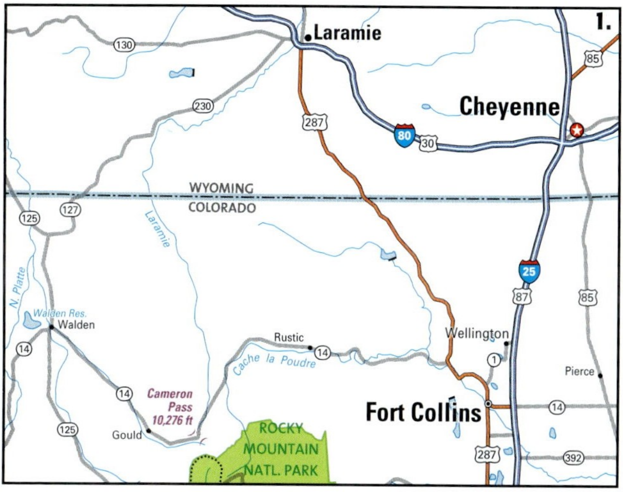
1.
Laramie
Cheyenne
Fort Collins
WYOMING
COLORADO
Walden Res.
Walden
Rustic
Cache la Poudre
Wellington
Pierce
Cameron Pass 10,276 ft
Gould
ROCKY MOUNTAIN NATL. PARK
Laramie
N. Platte
130
230
287
80
30
85
125
127
25
87
14
1
125
287
392

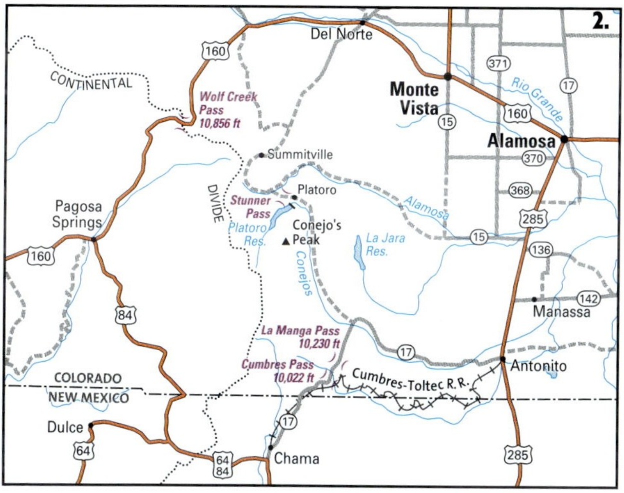
2.
Del Norte
CONTINENTAL
DIVIDE
Wolf Creek Pass 10,856 ft
Monte Vista
Alamosa
Rio Grande
Summitville
Platoro
Stunner Pass
Platoro Res.
Conejo's Peak
Conejos
Alamosa
La Jara Res.
Pagosa Springs
Manassa
La Manga Pass 10,230 ft
Cumbres Pass 10,022 ft
Cumbres-Toltec R.R.
Antonito
COLORADO
NEW MEXICO
Dulce
Chama
160
371
17
15
370
368
285
136
142
84
17
64
64 84
285

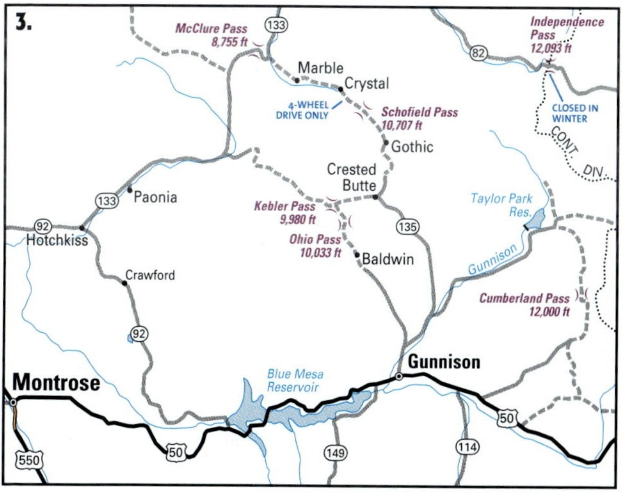
3.
McClure Pass 8,755 ft
Independence Pass 12,093 ft
Marble
Crystal
4-WHEEL DRIVE ONLY
Schofield Pass 10,707 ft
Gothic
CLOSED IN WINTER
CONT. DIV.
Crested Butte
Paonia
Hotchkiss
Kebler Pass 9,980 ft
Ohio Pass 10,033 ft
Baldwin
Taylor Park Res.
Gunnison
Crawford
Cumberland Pass 12,000 ft
Gunnison
Montrose
Blue Mesa Reservoir
133
82
133
92
135
92
50
550
50
149
114

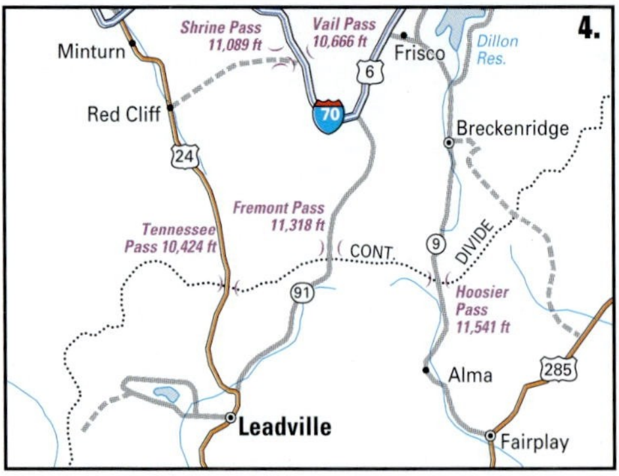
4.
Minturn
Shrine Pass
11,089 ft
Vail Pass
10,666 ft
Frisco
Dillon
Res.
6
Red Cliff
70
Breckenridge
24
Fremont Pass
11,318 ft
Tennessee
Pass 10,424 ft
CONT.
DIVIDE
9
91
Hoosier
Pass
11,541 ft
Alma
285
Leadville
Fairplay

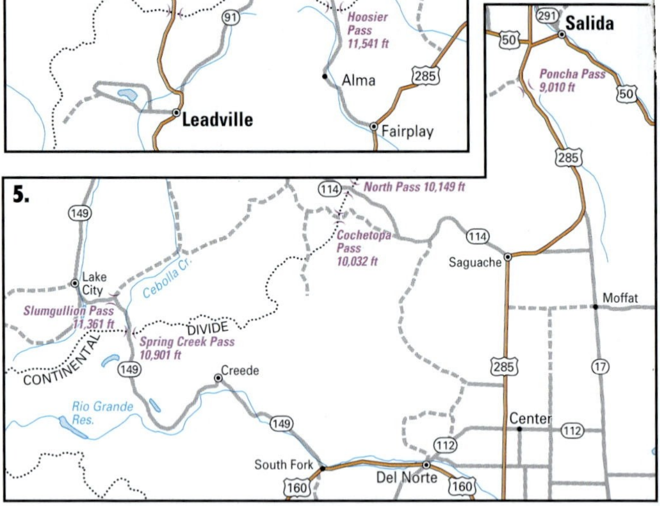
Salida
291
50
Poncha Pass
9,010 ft
50
285
5.
114
North Pass 10,149 ft
149
Cochetopa
Pass
10,032 ft
114
Saguache
Lake
City
Cebolla Cr.
Moffat
Slumgullion Pass
11,361 ft
DIVIDE
Spring Creek Pass
10,901 ft
CONTINENTAL
149
Creede
285
17
Rio Grande
Res.
149
Center
112
112
South Fork
160
Del Norte
160

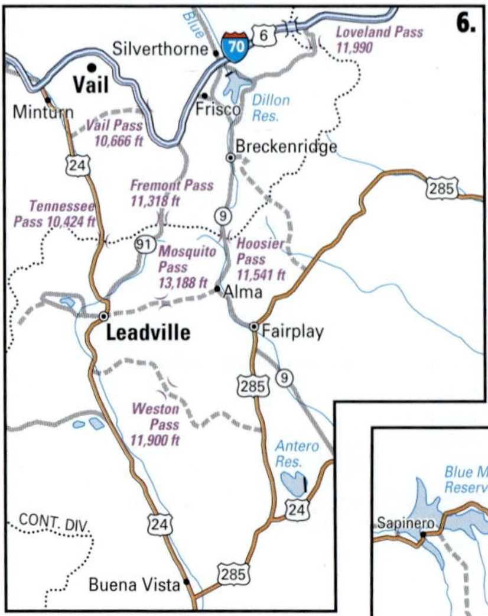
6.
Blue
Silverthorne
70
6
Loveland Pass
11,990
Vail
Minturn
Frisco
Dillon
Res.
Vail Pass
10,666 ft
Breckenridge
24
285
Fremont Pass
11,318 ft
Tennessee
Pass 10,424 ft
9
91
Mosquito
Pass
13,188 ft
Hoosier
Pass
11,541 ft
Alma
Leadville
Fairplay
9
285
Weston
Pass
11,900 ft
Antero
Res.
24
CONT. DIV.
24
285
Buena Vista

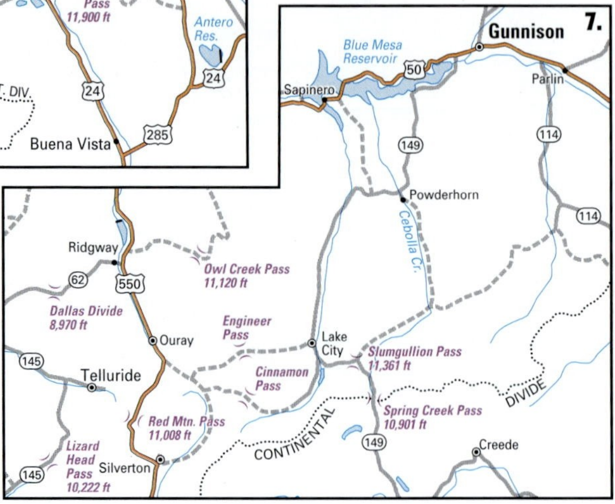
7.
Gunnison
Blue Mesa
Reservoir
50
Sapinero
Parlin
149
114
Powderhorn
114
Cebolla Cr.
Ridgway
Owl Creek Pass
11,120 ft
62
550
Dallas Divide
8,970 ft
Engineer
Pass
Ouray
Lake
City
145
Slumgullion Pass
11,361 ft
Telluride
Cinnamon
Pass
DIVIDE
Spring Creek Pass
10,901 ft
Red Mtn. Pass
11,008 ft
CONTINENTAL
149
Creede
Lizard
Head
Pass
10,222 ft
145
Silverton